A
Treasury of Children's Verse

Poems and Rhymes for the Very Young

A Treasury of Children's Verse

Poems and Rhymes for the Very Young

First published in 2021 Copyright © Stella Durndell 2021.

All rights reserved.

Other poetry books by this author: -

Life Love and Funny stuff
More Life Love and Funny Stuff
Even More Life Love and Funny Stuff

Acknowledgements

This book is dedicated to my daughters Laura and Amy and all the Pre-School children I had the pleasure of working with for over sixteen years, for being my inspiration.

A special thank you to Peter for bringing my poems to life with his amazing illustrations.

Hi,

I'm a mum of two grown up daughters and I live in Oxfordshire with my husband and my cat. I was born and raised in a small Buckinghamshire village and I'm definitely a country girl at heart.

I started writing poetry in 2010, mostly for my own pleasure. Then I began posting some of my poems on a poetry website and was amazed and delighted at the positive feedback I received. I continued writing more until I decided to publish them and I have three books of poems now published, this is my fourth book.

In 2017 I retired from working as a Pre-School Assistant, (sixteen and a half very happy years!) working with children aged two to four. I enjoyed it immensely and learned an enormous amount during that time.

Working with young children gives endless pleasure and inspiration for poetry. Every day was different, children come out with the most hilarious things and they're often very entertaining. We had books of poems which we read and I got to thinking that maybe I could write some new poems for younger children, so here we are.

Thank you for buying my book and I hope you and your children enjoy reading my poems and rhymes as much as I enjoyed writing them.

I continue to write poems for a fifth book which I hope to publish later this year.

Best wishes to you all and thank you.

Stella. x

Contents

A Pet to Love

I don't want a pet that slithers
I don't want pets that hiss
I want one warm and cuddly
That I can hug and kiss.

I don't want a pet that's scaly
Or a fish that I can't touch
I don't really think I'd want a pet
Like that very much.

I don't want a pet with feathers
Or any pet that lives in a cage
I want a little puppy
That I can train how to behave.

Or a kitten I can play with
It can sleep up in my room
I can't wait for a pet to love
I hope I can have one soon.

Building Dens

I'm going to build a shop

A shopkeeper I will be

I'll sell all my things

To everyone I see.

I'm going to build a police station

A policeman I will be

I'll look out for the baddies

And I'll arrest any that I see.

I'm going to build a wigwam

A Red Indian I will be

I'll use my bow and arrows

On any cowboys that I see.

I'm going to build a fire station

A firefighter I will be

I'll go and put out fires

And rescue anyone I see.

I'm going to build a surgery

A doctor I will be

I'll make everybody better

I'll help the patients that I see.

I'm going to build a rocket ship

An astronaut I will be

I'll say hello to the aliens

And I'll invite them back for tea.

Splish, Splash, Splosh!

Splish, splash, splosh in the puddles I go

Splishing and sploshing is so much fun.

Splish, splash, splosh through the puddles I go

Splishing and splashing everyone.

Splish, splash, splosh in the puddles I go

Mummy's calling, now I'd better run!

Cloud Watching

I'm lying on my back
On the green, green grass
Laying in the sun
Watching clouds drift past.

Look there's a whale
With its mouth open wide
If it goes much faster
Others will be sucked inside.

That one looks like an elephant
Although its trunk's a bit short
And there's a knight in shining armour
With battles to be fought.

There's a fluffy rabbit
With its ears so long
And there's a little bird
Tweeting out a song.

There's nothing that I'd rather do
On a sunny day
Than watch the clouds go by
As on the grass I lay.

I Can't Wait for Christmas

I can't wait for Father Christmas to come
I don't think I've been too naughty
I tidy away my toys every day
And I hope Father Christmas can see.
I help mummy in the kitchen
Putting plates and dishes away
I can go to the toilet on my own now
And I clean my teeth every day.
I remember to say please and thank you
I am ever so polite
I make my bed in the morning
And say my prayers every night.
I play nicely with my little brother
Even when he's messed up my game
And when he's been really naughty
I sometimes take the blame.
I help daddy in the garden
Putting up the Christmas lights
And I help mummy decorate the Christmas tree
Getting ready for Christmas night.
So, you see Father Christmas
I've been really good this year
And I've left sherry and a mince pie for you
And some carrots for your reindeer.

Lucy and Me

Hip, hip, hooray! It's my birthday
And today I am turning three.
My little sister Lucy
Is much smaller than me.

She is one and I am three
But it won't stay like that for long.
Because when she gets to three
I'll be five and big and strong.

I'll always be bigger than Lucy
She will always be smaller than me.
And even when we are grown up
Her big brother I'll always be.

If I Were...

If I were a rabbit I'd go hop, hop, hop

And no-one would make me stop, stop, stop.

If I were a cow, I'd go moo, moo, moo

Because there's nothing else, I'd rather do, do, do.

If I were a crocodile I'd go snap, snap, snap

Until it was time for a nap, nap, nap.

If I were a sheep, I'd go baa, baa, baa

And I'd look to see where the other sheep are, are, are.

If I were a horse, I'd go neigh, neigh, neigh

I'd only stop to eat my hay, hay, hay.

If I were a lion, I'd go roar, roar, roar

And if I was told to stop, I'd do it more, more, more.

If I were a duck, I'd go quack, quack, quack

All along the river and back, back, back.

But I'm a little boy, sitting on my favourite seat

Hoping that it's time for me to eat, eat, eat.

Pre-School

I like going to Pre-School

My friends are always there

We have stories and singing

Or play hairdressers brushing hair.

Sometimes we play doctors

And pretend someone is ill

And wrap them up in bandages

If only they'd keep still.

I like to play with playdough

Cooking lots of lovely food

And I might play with the farmyard

If I'm in the mood.

We have water and building blocks

I make castles in the sand

But I really like painting

I love to paint my hands.

Then make a handprint picture

For my Mum and Dad

Yet another piece of artwork,

I know that they'll be glad!

A Rainbow of Colours

Red is the ruby red poppy growing in the fields

Orange is a sweet satsuma ready to be peeled

Yellow is a golden sunflower swaying in the breeze

Green is the grass, the bushes and the trees

Blue is the summer sky, clouds drifting overhead

Indigo is the dark night sky when we are in our beds

Violet is a tiny flower to which bees love to fly.

This is a rainbow of colours arching across the sky.

Soda

I met a little pony
Soda is his name
His coat is a lovely dark brown
And he has a jet-black mane.

He is very calm and patient
And is good with children too
He tries his best to understand
What they want him to do.

He used to work at a riding school
Helping children to learn how to ride
He can be a little bit lazy and
Works better with someone at his side.

He loves having his coat brushed
And having his mane combed through
He also loves eating pony nuts
But he must only have a few.

He has such a gentle nature
You cannot help but love him
He'll nuzzle up for a pat and a stroke
And you just can't help but give in.

The Robins

I watched a pair of Robins make a nest in a hole in a wall

I couldn't see it very well 'cos I'm not very tall

They hopped around the garden, collecting dried moss and grass

Until they were happy that they'd finished it at last.

A few weeks later I watched them on the bird table eating seed

My mum said that it looked like they had baby Robins to feed

They hopped about finding juicy worms for their brood

They were very busy, backwards and forwards with all that food.

On a sunny day I heard some twittering by the wall

Four baby Robins with their parents with reassuring calls

They each flapped their wings and flew down to a wooden seat

Their mum and dad joined them and gave them worms to eat.

Through the summer and winter, the Robins weren't far away

I could hear them singing in the garden on and off during the day

I sprinkled birdseed on the lawn, they'd eat as brave as can be

Because as I got used to feeding them, they got used to me.

But Why?

Why are trees so tall?

Why is the sky so blue?

Why are bunny's ears so long?

Why am I smaller than you?

Why are mountains so high?

Why can't I fly like a bee?

Why is the sun so hot?

Why are you bigger than me?

Why is spaghetti so wiggly?

Why can't I eat a lemon?

Why am I only five and a half

And you're big now you're seven?

The Tooth Fairies

The Tooth Fairies are busy
As they are every night
Searching for those pearly teeth
Which are hidden out of sight.

They fly around silently
Under pillows they feel around
Swapping lost teeth with money
Without making any sound.

Sometimes they have to hunt harder
In a tooth box or in a tin
But if it's there they'll find it
No matter where it's hiding.

But if by chance the tooth is still there
In the morning, leave it be
For the fairies will return the next night
When they're not quite so busy.

Because Tooth Fairies make jewellery
Precious bracelets for their arms
And dainty little necklaces
From which to hang their charms.

A, B, C Rhyme

A is for apple
B is for ball
C is for cat
D is for door
E is for elephant
F is for fan
G is for garden
H is for hand
I is for ice cream
J is for jam
K is for koala
L is for lamb
M is for mummy
N is for nail
O is for orange
P is for pail
Q is for queen
R is for rat
S is for stream
T is for tap
U is for umbrella
V is for van
W is for window
X is for exam
Y is for you and
Z is for zoo
Now see if you can think of some too!

Be Like Animals

Bounce like a kangaroo; bounce, bounce, bounce
Then pounce like a lion; pounce, pounce, pounce.

Go snap like a crocodile; snap, snap, snap
And nap like a dormouse; nap, nap, nap.

Jump like a rabbit; jump, jump, jump
Then trumpet like an elephant; trump, trump, trump.

Moo like a cow; moo, moo, moo
And oooh like a monkey; oooh, oooh, oooh.

Creep like a cat; creep, creep, creep
Then leap like a frog; leap, leap, leap.

Fly high like an eagle; fly, fly, fly
Try to waddle like a penguin; try, try, try.

Roar like a tiger; roar, roar, roar
Now see if you can think of any more, more, more.

The Easter Bunny

The Easter Bunny will be visiting soon

Skipping and singing a merry tune

With his long, soft ears and a snuffly nose

I don't know where he comes from or where he goes

But if I'm good he comes once a year

No-one has seen him but I know that he's near

Chocolate eggs he leaves as a trail

Then off he goes with a twitch of his tail.

One, Two, Three, Four, Five

One, two, three, four, five

I saw some bees buzzing around a hive.

Six, seven, eight, nine, ten

Some went in and came out again.

Where do you think they go?

Anywhere that flowers grow.

And what do you think they do?

They make honey for me and you.

I Want to be a Dinosaur

When I grow up, I want to be a dinosaur

Because dinosaurs are cool

They don't have to do what anyone says

And they don't have to go to school.

I'll be a Tyrannosaurus Rex with sharp teeth

And I'll eat sweets and ice cream all day

I'll be scary and I'll roar a lot

I'll make everyone run away.

Or I could be a huge Brontosaurus

With a great big, enormous long neck

I wouldn't want to be scary though

I'd reach things short people can't get.

I'd quite like to be a Triceratops

With three huge horns on my head

I'd give rides to all of my school friends

In return they'd make sure I was fed.

Maybe I'd be a fierce Velociraptor

Chasing people around all day

I'd run very, very fast to catch them

Then I'd ask if they wanted to play.

I think being a dinosaur could be lots of fun

Although I don't know if I'd have many friends

And I might be too big to live in my house

And I might break things for dad to mend.

It's Snowing Again!

It's a snow day, hooray! that means we can play

Outside all day, come with us!

It's sunny and bright and the snow's glistening white

It's cold yes, but don't make a fuss!

There are snowballs to make and photos to take

Of all of our snowy creations

We'll keep going all day 'til the snow goes away

This is better than any Playstation.

A snowman, his wife and his children

A snow dog, a shark and a cat

We find twigs and leaves and stones of course

For embellishment; and a scarf and a hat.

We make the biggest snowballs our little hands can hold

And throw them at each other with glee

We squeal with delight when we hit our targets

I squealed with pain when they hit me.

Bored now we decide to make snow angels

Each laying down on the fluffy soft snow

Extending and flapping our arms and legs

Wanting our angel to be the best one on show.

We jump up, our cold faces glowing

Our freezing hands now throbbing with pain

We decide to go in, warm up and dry off

Then we'll go out and do it all again.

My Holiday

I'm going on holiday soon to somewhere warm and sunny

It must be nice because mummy said it cost a lot of money

We're going in an aeroplane, high up in the sky

I'll look out of the window and see the clouds go by.

There's a great big swimming pool with a slide that looks like fun

And lots of beds with towels on to lay out in the sun

There's a lovely beach with soft white sand for making castles on

Until the tide comes in and my castle will be gone.

The food is really yummy, we can have whatever we choose

Mummy says when we get home some weight she'll have to lose

After dinner there's a disco, lots of children get up and dance

If they want to win a prize, then this is their chance.

There's sometimes a singer, and sometimes they're quite good

I'd like to go up and sing, if I was allowed I would

But it's usually late by this time and up we go to our room

Tomorrow we'll go to a water park and we'll whizz down all the flumes.

Questions, Questions

Why does the sun come out in the day

And the moon comes out at night?

Why is my Dad so heavy

When he says that I'm so light?

Why do girls wear pink and boys wear blue?

It doesn't make any sense.

Why is a pound coin smaller

Than a silver fifty pence?

How does a giraffe have seven neck bones

The same as a tiny mouse?

Why does the Queen live in a palace

And I live in a house?

Why is the grass so green

And holly berries are so red?

Why am I never tired

When Mum says it's time for bed?

The Chicken's Box

I don't know what's a chicken's box
Is it where they lay their eggs?
My Mum said that I'd got them
When I got out of bed.

I don't know why a chicken
Would lay its eggs on me
But I don't like it very much
They really are itchy.

I've got so many spots
They are everywhere
On my tummy and my face
And even in my hair.

Well, the chicken can have its box back
I don't want it anymore
And if it isn't for laying eggs in
I don't know what it's for.

The Seaside

I love to go to the seaside
And make castles in the sand
I like doing it by myself
But I let Daddy lend a hand.

We make windows out of shells
And make towers and a moat
And when it fills with water
I can sail my little boat.

I like playing in the rock pools
And I dip in my green net
I want to catch a dolphin
But I haven't caught one yet.

I paddle in the foamy sea
Holding Mummy and Daddy's hands
As the waves come in, they swing me
Up and over, then back on the sand.

I really like the seaside
Everyone is having fun
But my favourite bit is our picnic
On a blanket in the sun.

Weather Changes

One day in the summer the sky was blue

An hour later there were clouds, and quite a few

After an hour the sky turned grey

Another hour passed and down came the rain

Whilst it was raining the sun came through

And made a beautiful rainbow too.

Bedtime

Mummy says it's time for bed

But zillions of thoughts are racing through my head

Of monsters, aliens, kings and queens

I imagine where they're going and where they've been.

A doctor, a vet, a nurse, a farmer

A princess and a knight in shining armour

My thoughts are having a party in my head

Whilst I'm tucked up in my cosy bed.

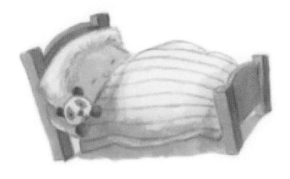

Chat, Chat, Chat!

When we're at the school gate
And I just want to go
My Mum's always chatting
It makes me moan
I want to go home!

When I'm playing at a friend's house
And I don't want to stay
My Mum's always chatting
It makes me say
I want to go home!

When we are at the play area
And I have had enough
My Mum's always chatting
It gets me in a huff
I want to go home!

When we are out shopping
Trying to buy some food
My Mum's always chatting
It gets me in a mood
I want to go home!

Five Little Mice

Five little mice went scampering away
All they wanted to do was play
One little mouse got caught in a trap
And four little mice came scampering back.

Four little mice went scampering away
All they wanted to do was play
One little mouse got caught in a trap
And three little mice came scampering back.

Three little mice went scampering away
All they wanted to do was play
One little mouse got caught in a trap
And two little mice came scampering back.

Two little mice went scampering away
All they wanted to do was play
One little mouse got caught in a trap
And one little mouse came scampering back.

One little mouse went scampering away
All he wanted to do was play
But that little mouse got caught in a trap
So, no little mice came scampering back.

I Want to Be…

I want to be an eagle; I'd fly up so high
That I could almost touch the clouds in the sky.

I want to be a killer whale, I'd swim the oceans blue
I'd be so scary no-one would tell me what to do.

I want to be a tiger, in the jungle I would hide
I'd roar my scariest roar and open my mouth wide.

I want to be a horse, I'd while away my day
With other horses in the fields, munching on some hay.

I want to be a cat; I'd play and sleep and eat
And I'd jump up on the laps of everyone I meet.

I want to be an elephant with great big flappy ears
I'd have a brilliant memory; I'd remember things for years.

I want to be a dog; in the park I would run
Playing with a ball would be lots of fun.

But I'm a little girl with lots of things inside my head
And now I'm really tired and I'm getting into bed.

Just Five Minutes More

Just five minutes more, Mum
Just five minutes more.
I'll help with the dishes and I'll mop the floor
Please, just five minutes more.

Just five minutes more, Mum
Just five minutes more.
I'll put away my toys, I won't be untidy anymore
Please, just five minutes more.

Just five minutes more, Mum
Just five minutes more.
I'll eat all my vegetables and even ask for more
Please, just five minutes more.

Just five minutes more, Mum
Just five minutes more.
After school I'll get my ball and play outdoors
Please, just five minutes more.

Just five minutes more, Mum
Just five minutes more.
I promise I'll do all of my chores
Please, just five minutes more.

Just five minutes more, Mum
Just five minutes more.
I don't want to go to bed yet
Please, just five minutes more.
Please?

My Nannie

I really miss my Nannie

I saw her every day

But she was very poorly

And had to go away.

I think she's gone to Heaven

Because she was kind and good

And if I was ever sad

She always understood.

I really miss her cuddles

And the games we used to play

But as long as I remember her

In my heart she'll always stay.

Opposites

On top of the table
And under the chair.
Up the hill
And down the stairs.

In the door
And out of the gate.
On time
And now very late.

As big as an elephant
As small as a mouse.
As short as a daisy
As tall as a house.

Over the bridge
Now under it too.
Lots of sweets
Now only a few.

As hot as a summer's day
As cold as ice.
Someone being horrible
Now someone being nice.

As dark as night
As light as day.
As quiet as a mouse
Noisy children at play.

Rabbit

I have a little rabbit who sleeps in a hutch

Mummy doesn't really like it very much.

When we let him in the garden

He digs up all the flowers.

Mummy gets cross because

To plant them took her hours!

When I'm Big

When I'm big I want to drive a tractor on a farm

Or be a policeman with a radio, keeping folks from harm.

I want to be a doctor, making people better

Or a postman with a mail van, delivering you a letter.

I'd like to be a teacher, with glasses like Miss Mires

Or a firefighter with a hose, saving people from fires.

I like animals, so I'd be a vet, looking after dogs and cats

Or I could just be a mummy, and have cups of tea and chats.

Sweeties

I love to go to the sweet shop
To spend some pennies on sweets
It's so hard to decide
When it's full of yummy treats.

Hmm now do I feel like Smarties
Or toffees that are chewy?
Or M&Ms or Maltesers
Or something caramel and gooey?

I think I might get some liquorice
And a Milky Bar so white
Or maybe some pear drops
But they're so difficult to bite.

I know, I'll get Fruit Pastilles
And some Jelly Babies too
And a little Freddo chocolate
I think that will do.

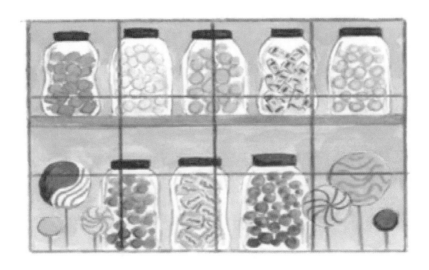

The Summer Holidays

We've broken up from school today
I think we're going to Spain
Six whole weeks to have some fun
I hope it doesn't rain.

We're going to a castle
To see a real knight
I wonder if he'll kill a dragon
I really think he might.

Then we're going to a safari park
To see the animals being fed
I don't think we can feed them
They might eat us instead.

We're going to a funfair
On the roundabouts and slides
I like the teacups and helter-skelter
But not the bigger, faster rides.

But I really like to stay home too
And build dens and make cakes with mummy
We have a tea party with my toys
They think my cakes are yummy!

The Naughty Step

I'm sitting on the naughty step
And I don't know what I've done
Mummy has made me sit here
She always spoils my fun.

I only took my little sister Chloe's
Favourite car
I would play with mine
But I don't know where they are.

So here I am again
On the step I know so well
Because I sit here every time
I make my sister yell.

I try to play nicely
But I sometimes get too rough
And mummy ends up shouting
That she has had enough.

Ten Little Children

Ten little children lined up to have a swim
But one couldn't wait and jumped right in!

Nine little children lined up to have a swim
But one couldn't wait and jumped right in!

Eight little children lined up to have a swim
But one couldn't wait and jumped right in!

Seven little children lined up to have a swim
But one couldn't wait and jumped right in!

Six little children lined up to have a swim
But one couldn't wait and jumped right in!

Five little children lined up to have a swim
But one couldn't wait and jumped right in!

Four little children lined up to have a swim
But one couldn't wait and jumped right in!

Three little children lined up to have a swim
But one couldn't wait and jumped right in!

Two little children lined up to have a swim
But one couldn't wait and jumped right in!

One child left alone waiting for a swim
But because he was lonely, he jumped right in!

Brock the Badger

Brock the badger prowls at night
Even when the snow falls thick and white.
His beautiful fur stands out in the snow
Wherever he travels, wherever he goes.

He lives in a sett deep down in the ground
Where no-one can hear him, not a sound.
The sett is warm and cosy inside
High and long and very wide.

Brock's short legs shuffle quickly along
Even though they are short, they are very strong.
He snouts around in the dark finding grubs to eat
Then in the day he goes to sleep.

Christmas is Coming

Christmas is coming soon
And my mum will always say
That if I'm very naughty
Santa won't come with his sleigh.

So, I try to be really good
I'm kind and helpful too
I eat up all my dinner
And say please and thank you.

I always tidy away my toys
And if not straight away
My mum has to remind me
And I tidy at the end of the day.

I'm really worried that Santa won't come
With his reindeer on Christmas Eve
I try to be good, I really do
I hope some presents he'll leave.

I'll be nice to my little brother
I won't tease him or make him cry
I'll share my favourite toys with him
Please Santa don't pass me by.

Christmas Eve is here at last
I can't wait to go to bed
I screw my eyes shut tightly
With jingling bells filling my head.

Santa thank you, thank you
A sack of presents by my door
Can I be a little bit naughty now
'Till next Christmas, when I want some more?

The Playground

On the slide I climb up and slide down

On the roundabout I whizz around and around

On the climbing frame I go so high I nearly reach the sky

I lay on the grass and watch the clouds drift by

On the swings I go backwards and forwards all day

And when it's time to go, I just want to stay

But my tummy tells me it's time for tea

And mummy will soon come calling me.

Go Outside and Play!

One, two, three, four, five

Find a box and sit inside

Six, seven, eight, nine, ten

Let's pretend that it's a den.

Eenie, meenie, miney, mo,

Pretend it's a rocket and away we go!

One, two, three, four, five

Play with the water, see the fish dive

Six, seven, eight, nine, ten

Empty the bottles, fill them up again.

Eenie, meenie, miney, mo,

Make some boats and watch them go!

One, two, three, four, five

Climb up the steps and down the slide

Six, seven, eight, nine, ten

Swing high on the swing and down again.

Eenie, meenie, miney, mo,

Climb the climbing frame, how high can you go?

One, two, three, four, five

Get on your bike and go for a ride

Six, seven eight, nine, ten

When it's time for tea, come home again.

Eenie, meenie, miney, mo,

Water the garden, help the flowers grow!

Who Should I Ask?

When I ask my Mum

She'll sometimes say

"We'll talk about it another day."

When I ask my Dad

He'll always say

"Ask your mother, I'm too busy today."

When I ask my Grandma

She'll always say

"Of course, you can dear.

But don't tell your parents... Okay?"

The Swing

I love the swing in my garden
It hangs from a great big tree
And when I swing really high
I can see what a bird can see.

I can see the church across the fields
And the sails on the windmill going around
If I kick my legs out even more
I can go even higher I've found.

There are rabbits sitting in the sun
And there are cars going down the lane
Someone is riding a lovely brown horse
The wind is blowing its mane.

I love my swing more than anything
Over walls and hedges I can see
But I can't stay on it for ever
Because it's nearly time for tea.

If I Could Be…

If I could be an animal……

That animal would be

A great big blue whale swimming in the sea.

Or a lion in the sunshine living on the plains

Or a cuddly koala eating leaves from bamboo canes.

Or an enormous elephant with great big flappy ears

Or a terrifying tiger who everybody fears.

Or I could be an eagle soaring way up high

Or maybe an albatross gliding across the sky.

But if I could be anything, anything at all

I'd be a big T-Rex 'cos he's the fiercest of them all.

Roar!!

Learning my Letters

A, B, C, D, E

I'm learning my alphabet, learn with me!

F, G, H, I, J

I'm learning new letters every day

K, L, M, N, O, P

Come along you'll learn with me

Q, R, S, T, U, V

We're nearly there as you can see

W, X, Y and Z

I'm tired now, I'm off to bed.

My Pussy Cat

I love my little pussy cat

I like to smell her fur

I stroke her very gently

Because I like to hear her purr.

She loves to lay on piles of clothes

And covers them with hair

Sometimes she'll stretch out on my bed

Or even on a chair.

When I'm asleep she touches me

Very gently with her paw

Instead of using her cat flap

She likes me to open the door.

She would never hurt me

And I'm as gentle as can be

I love my little pussy cat

And I know that she loves me.

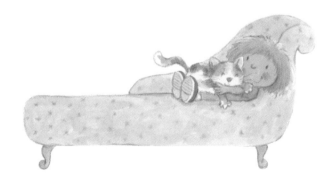

Party Time

I'm going to a party
My friends will all be there
We'll wear our pretty dresses
And ribbons in our hair.

We'll do a pass the parcel
And musical statues too
Standing still when the music stops
Is really hard to do.

We all run around for musical chairs
And then it's time to eat
We sit up to the table
And eye up all the treats.

There are sandwiches in triangles
Sausage rolls and cubes of cheese
Cucumber and carrot sticks
We could have anything we pleased.

Then cup cakes with coloured icing
Chocolate fingers and party rings
Then birthday cake with candles lit
And everybody sings.

The birthday girl blew the candles out
In one almighty puff
She wanted to blow them again and again
But was told that twice was enough.

We sat in a circle and watched
Whilst presents were unwrapped
And soon it was time to go home
With a balloon and a party bag.

One, Two, Three

One, two, go to the zoo

Three, four, draw a dinosaur

Five six, build with bricks

Seven, eight, shut the gate

Nine, ten, draw with your pens

Eleven, twelve, seek and delve

Thirteen, fourteen, shake your tambourine

Fifteen, sixteen, go and see the Queen

Seventeen, eighteen, always use sunscreen

Nineteen, twenty make sure you use plenty!

Santa's Story

Santa said to his reindeer
"Come on you lot, we have a busy night ahead
Delivering Christmas presents
To boys and girls asleep in their beds!"

The reindeer went, pulling Santa and his sleigh
Through the dark night's sky
Over mountains, rivers and forests
Seeing for miles from up so high.

Landing gently on the rooftops
And with the help of fairy dust
Santa slipped down the chimneys
With his sack fit to bust.

He quietly left some presents
For every girl and boy
Books, puzzles and games
So many different toys.

Stopping for a mince pie gift
He quickly returned to his sleigh
And off they went, no time to lose
It would soon be Christmas Day!

The Owl

The owl sat up high in the tree

He looked down and he spotted me.

"Hello Mister Owl, do you want to come and play?

If you don't, I can come back another day."

He ignored me and flew off on silent wing

To hunt and see what he could bring

For his babies waiting in his nest,

Mice and voles, they liked the best.

They would wait patiently for their meal

But as soon as he was back, they would loudly squeal.

Each wanting to get more food

Than the rest of the hungry brood.

"Goodbye Mister Owl," I waved and said.

"It's time for *me* to go home and be fed."

A Snow Day!

I don't want to go to school today

It's been snowing, I want to stay home and play

I want to build a snowman as big as my dad

With a big smiley face, I don't want him to look sad.

I'll make snow angels in all the fresh new snow

And make a big pile of snowballs all ready to throw

I'll play outside until my fingers are so cold

And my hands hurt so much there's nothing I can hold.

I'm having fun, I don't want to go inside

But my throbbing fingers help me to decide

So, I'll go indoors and I'll dry off and warm up

And have hot chocolate in my favourite cup.

"Little children are a treasure,
Their worth you cannot measure."

Ron Zupsic

Printed in Great Britain
by Amazon